About this book

Robben Island – Symbol of Resistance is a history of Robben Island. But it is also a tribute to the many people who were imprisoned there, kept apart from society, separated not only by chains, high prison walls and asylum doors, but also by the stretch of icy water which divides Robben Island from the mainland. In particular, it is a tribute to those prisoners who spent so many years isolated from the rest of society because of their political beliefs and their untiring struggle against apartheid in South Africa.

When the last political prisoners were released from Robben Island in 1991, they gave some of their prison possessions to the Mayibuye Centre. They wanted to help others to understand and remember the life of prisoners on the island through these objects – articles of clothing, personal treasures, things they read and wrote, and things they made. These objects make up the Apple-Box Archives (named after the apple boxes which prisoners used to carry their possessions when they left Robben Island on their way to freedom). This book is dedicated to those prisoners, and to the many others who died in the island prison.

Robben Island – Symbol of Resistance was developed and is co-published by SACHED Books and Mayibuye Books. The book grew out of the widely acclaimed *Esiqithini: The Robben Island Exhibition* which was co-produced by the Mayibuye Centre and the South African Museum in 1993.

About SACHED Books

SACHED Books is the book publishing division of the SACHED Trust, a national non-profit organisation, dedicated to educational development. The major focus of SACHED's work is adult education, and this book is one of a series for adults, designed to encourage a culture of reading in South Africa.

About Mayibuye Books

Mayibuye Books is the book publishing division of the Mayibuye Centre at the University of the Western Cape. The Mayibuye Centre is a pioneering project helping to recover areas of South African history that have been neglected in the past. It also provides space for cultural creativity and expression in a way that promotes the process of change and reconstruction in a democratic South Africa.

Robben Island

Symbol of Resistance

Developed by Barbara Hutton

Commissioned and edited by Josie Egan
Copy-edited by Penny Nyren
Design consultant Graham Arbuckle
DTP conversion in 11/13 Palatino Roman by Andy Thesen
Cover design by Graham Arbuckle
Illustrations by Ian Lusted, Muhdni Grimwood and Mara Singer
Commissioned photographs by Tracey Derrick
Picture research Karen Korte

Published by SACHED Books, PO Box 11350, Johannesburg 2000, South Africa,
and
Mayibuye Books, UWC, Private Bag X17, Bellville 7535, South Africa

Mayibuye History and Literature Series No. 51

Second impression 1997
© SACHED
ISBN 0 86877 417 0

Printed and bound by CTP Book Printers (Pty) Ltd, Caxton Street, Parow 7500, Cape Town

R6644/RM5449

Contents

Acknowledgements

The publishers and author would like to thank everyone who contributed to the development of this book.

In particular we thank: the staff at the South African Museum who co-developed and hosted the *Esiqithini: The Robben Island Exhibition* together with the Mayibuye Centre in 1993; the staff at the South African Library for their assistance in locating many of the photographs and illustrations; Sedick Isaacs for his assistance in identifying the different buildings in the prison illustration on pages 46–47; Achmat Davids for his comments on the section dealing with Eastern prisoners on Robben Island; Leslie Witz for his valuable comments and suggestions and Peace Visions for their assistance.

The Mayibuye Centre would also like to thank the Royal Netherlands Embassy for its assistance in sponsoring this publication.

Introduction

We, that is the Rivonia group (Mandela, Mbeki, Sisulu, Kathrada, Mhlaba, Mlangeni and Motsoaledi), arrived on Robben Island on the 13th of June 1964. It was a Saturday – cold, windy, raining. We cannot forget the first months at the quarry where we mined stone – we came back with blisters, bloody hands and sore muscles. And we cannot forget the dozen years or more when we were forced to sleep on the cold cement floors with three blankets and a thin sisal mat. Also we cannot forget the cold showers for 13 or 14 years. There is much more that one can recall, much more that we have found in ourselves to forgive, but these we will never forget.

Someone has written about two prisoners looking out of their cell window: The one saw iron bars while the other saw stars. How true. The very fact of being in prison means that you are deprived of certain things, the main one being the loss of your freedom. But once you have come to terms with the things that you cannot change, you start making adjustments and where possible you change the environment to make the stay less intolerable.

The real picture of prison life is a picture of great warmth, fellowship, friendship, humour and laughter, of strong convictions, of generosity of spirit, of compassion, solidarity and care. It is a picture of continuous learning, of getting to know and live with your fellow beings. But more important, it is where you come to know yourself, your weaknesses, inadequacies and your potential.

If I were to sum up in a few sentences our years in prison, I would say: While we will not forget the brutality of apartheid, we will not want Robben Island to be a monument to our hardship and suffering. We would want Robben Island to be a monument reflecting the triumph of the human spirit against the forces of evil. A triumph of freedom and human dignity over oppression and humiliation. A triumph of wisdom and largeness of spirit against small minds and pettiness. A triumph of courage and determination over human frailty and weakness. A triumph of non-racialism over bigotry and intolerance. A triumph of a new South Africa over the old. *Mr Ahmed 'Kathy' Kathrada opening Esiqithini: The Robben Island Exhibition, 26 May 1993.*

Robben Island is 4,5 km long and 1,5 km wide. It takes between 15 and 30 minutes to walk across the breadth of the island and between 90 minutes and 2 hours to walk right around it. The island is separated from the mainland by 9 km of sea and it takes between 30 and 40 minutes to travel to Robben Island by motorboat, today.

MINTO-HILL - THE HIGHEST POINT ON THE ISLAND

THE LIGHT HOUSE BUILT IN 1804

VAN RIEBEECK'S QUARRY

GRAVEYARD

THE GUEST HOUSE THIS USED TO BE WHERE THE COMMISSIONER OF THE ISLAND LIVED

OLD VICTORIAN BUILDING - TODAY THE ISLAND SCHOOL

THE ANGLICAN CHURCH, 1841

THE OLD LEPER MORGUE NOW USED AS A BANK

THE OLD MALE LEPER CHURCH, BUILT IN 1895. THERE ARE PLANS FOR THIS TO BECOME A PEACE CENTRE

SITE FORMER COLONY

CORRECTIONAL SERVICES FACILITY

FAURE JETTY

Robben Island

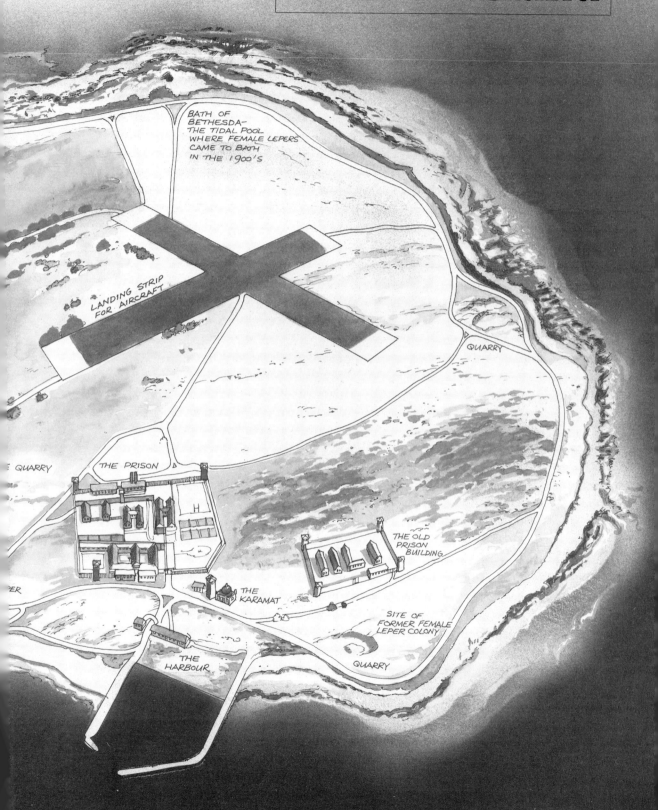

BATH OF
BETHESDA-
THE TIDAL POOL
WHERE FEMALE LEPERS
CAME TO BATH
IN THE 1900'S

LANDING STRIP
FOR AIRCRAFT

QUARRY

QUARRY

THE PRISON

THE OLD
PRISON
BUILDING

PER

THE KARAMAT

SITE OF
FORMER FEMALE
LEPER COLONY

QUARRY

THE
HARBOUR

Robben Island in the distance, with Cape Town in the foreground.

Robben Island is a small piece of land in Table Bay, only a few kilometres from the beaches of Bloubergstrand, the high blocks of flats at Mouille Point and the bustle of Cape Town's Waterfront. It is surrounded by the ice-cold Atlantic Ocean and has no protection from the strong winds of the Cape that constantly sweep across its rocky surface.

Over the last 500 years this wind-swept island has been used to isolate people from society. Prisoners and exiles have included slaves from Angola and West Africa, princes from the East, the chiefs who resisted British colonial rule, lepers, the insane, and leaders of the struggle against apartheid. Every time these prisoners looked out across the water from Robben Island to the mainland they were reminded of another world that continued there without them.

But Robben Island is not a place of defeat. Rather it is a symbol of political resistance, of great courage and of human dignity in the face of terrible suffering.

SECTION 1
Robben Island:
its early history

Not always an island

Today, Robben Island is completely surrounded by the Atlantic Ocean. But it has not always been an island. Millions of years ago Robben Island was linked to Bloubergstrand by a ridge of land. It looked like a small hill on the mainland, largely covered with dry grass. Wild animals such as elephants, lions and buck wandered freely between Bloubergstrand and the area that is the island today. Over the years the strong currents of the sea, the merciless winds and the rising and falling sea-levels changed the appearance of the island, until eventually it was completely cut off from the mainland, as it is today.

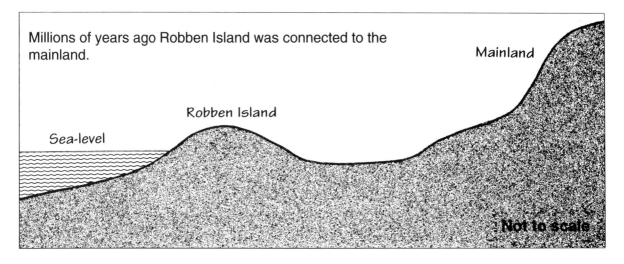

Millions of years ago Robben Island was connected to the mainland.

Mainland

Robben Island

Sea-level

Not to scale

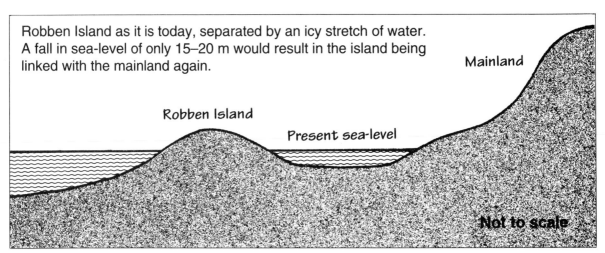

Robben Island as it is today, separated by an icy stretch of water. A fall in sea-level of only 15–20 m would result in the island being linked with the mainland again.

Mainland

Robben Island

Present sea-level

Not to scale

Meals for sailors

Five hundred years ago, European sailors who were on their way
to the East Indies stopped at the Cape to get fresh meat, vegetables
and water. Some of these explorers traded beads, spices and
metals with the Khoisan at the Cape, in return for cattle and sheep.
But others feared the Khoisan and preferred to stop on the little
island at the entrance to Table Bay – Robben Island. Here they
could hunt penguins, seals and tortoises for food.

--→ Bartolomeu Dias (1488)
→ Vasco da Gama (1498)

The European explorers

Explorers from
many countries in
Europe sailed
around the
southern tip of
Africa to get to the
East Indies. Here
they bought
cotton, silk and
spices which they
sold in Europe.
They used the
Cape as a half-way
point on these
voyages, to stop
and rest, and to
pick up fresh food
and water.

It took explorers 12 years to find a sea-route to India via the Cape.
Bartolomeu Dias first rounded the Cape in 1488. Ten years later Vasco
da Gama successfully reached India after sailing for almost a year. This
map shows the routes that these two explorers followed.

The explorers were not the first people to arrive at the Cape. The Khoisan had been living in Southern Africa for thousands of years. They had travelled from Botswana, hunting wild animals and gathering food from the veld. The Khoisan eventually settled at the Cape, where they farmed cattle and sheep.

Explorers traded with the Khoisan for fresh meat. But some explorers did not even bother to trade, they simply shot the Khoisan's cattle on sight. The Khoisan fought back, and over the next two hundred years this conflict between the Khoisan and the Europeans increased.

Robbe Eiland: a source of food

Some explorers feared the Khoisan of the mainland, calling them cannibals and refusing to trade with them. These explorers preferred to hunt for food on the island which the Dutch called Robbe Eiland, from the Dutch word for seal – *robbe*. This is how Robben Island got its name, from the thousands of seals which bred on the island at that time.

Over the next 200 years the wild animals of Robben Island were killed to provide meals for sailors. Unfortunately each European crew member who used the island as a hunting ground took a little more of its wildlife. A new source of food had to be found.

Trade between the Khoisan and the European sailors was not often a peaceful process.

In the 1600s a British sailor left eight sheep and two rams, that he had traded from the Khoisan, on Robben Island. He hoped that these animals would start breeding so that they could be used as a source of fresh meat by passing sailors. This tradition of leaving sheep to breed on the island continued, and for a long time it became a regular practice for sailors to leave thin sheep on the island in exchange for fatter ones.

Sailors visiting the island wrote about some of the animals they saw there:

In this island there is a great abundance of seales and penguines, in such numbers as is almost incredible. Sailor in 1591

Great numbers of sea-bears are found, which bleat like sheep, but are unlike them in taste, and for my part I could not eat them, nor the penguins, because they tasted of fish oil ... although most of our crew found them good and preferred them to bacon. Sailor in 1620

Some sailors drew pictures of the animals they saw. These were often very different to the animals they represented, like this drawing of a penguin, alongside, which dates back to 1626.

The beginnings of a prison

In the mid-1600s, one European trading nation, the Dutch, established their rule at the Cape and in the East Indies. But they soon found that the local people would not give in peacefully to Dutch rule. Many Khoisan of the Cape, princes, Muslim leaders and Muslim priests of the East Indies resisted Dutch rule. Some of these enemies of the Dutch were exiled to Robben Island and became its first political prisoners.

Dutch rule

Van Riebeeck was the representative of the Dutch East India Company at the Cape. He was sent to the Cape to establish a refreshment station where ships could get fresh supplies on their way to the East. Robben Island became more and more important to this refreshment station. Van Riebeeck was dependent on the Khoisan to provide the station with food. But often the Khoisan and the Dutch were in conflict. So the island became like a pantry, or food store, where people could get penguin eggs, meat, and seal skins and oil. Like others before him, Van Riebeeck also used the island as a sheep farm, and he placed shepherds on the island to look after the sheep.

The crew of the Dutch East India Company were relieved to see Table Mountain at last. The voyage from Europe had taken six months and they badly needed fresh provisions. As their captain steered the ship into Table Bay, he heard the cannon shot fired from Lion's Head signalling that a new ship had arrived.

Table Mountain

Lion's Head

Table Bay

In 1654 Van Riebeeck left some of his men on Robben Island under a supervisor called the Postholder. These men worked on the island searching for food, mining shale (a type of rock) and making lime. They also had to light signal fires and beacons to guide ships safely into Table Bay.

Signal fires were lit to guide ships safely into Table Bay.

The Castle.

The first industries at the Cape

Van Riebeeck established the first industries on Robben Island – the cutting of stone used for walls, roofs and stoeps in buildings on the mainland; and the burning of shells to make lime, which was used to make paint and plaster. Stone from Robben Island was used to build Cape Town's Castle.

Robben Island's first prisoners

Autshumato

A group of Khoisan who had no cattle of their own lived in Table Bay. The European explorers called them *strandlopers* or *watermen*. Their leader was a man named Autshumato, but the Europeans called him Harry. In the early 1600s the British took Autshumato to the East Indies. There he learnt to speak English, and when he returned he became the agent and postman for the British in Southern Africa.

Autshumato asked the British to let him and 20 of his followers live on Robben Island. His job on the island was to keep watch on all ships entering Table Bay and to light signal fires to attract sailors wishing to send or receive letters.

On Robben Island the strandlopers hunted penguins and seals which they thought were a delicacy. But within eight years they had destroyed most of the island's wildlife. In 1640 a Dutch sailor reported that 'there was nothing there but one penguin, and no wild beasts except a few seals ...'. So the island lost its attraction for the strandlopers and they returned to the mainland.

Many sailors used Robben Island as a post office. They left letters on the island, for passing ships to collect, usually in a secret spot under a specially marked rock, similar to the one above.

Strandlopers and Dutch explorers.

By the time Van Riebeeck arrived at the Cape, Autshumato was playing an important role as middle-man and translator between the Khoisan and the Dutch. But Van Riebeeck tended to blame him for any breakdown in trade with the Khoisan. Van Riebeeck believed that supplies would be cheaper and more plentiful with Autshumato out of the way.

In July 1658 Van Riebeeck imprisoned Autshumato and two other Khoisan on Robben Island. A year later Autshumato and his fellow prisoners managed to steal a small rowing boat and make a daring escape. Two weeks later the Dutch found the boat safe on the mainland. It seems that nothing could stop this amazing character.

We are half afraid that the aforesaid Harry — being very much attached to the Saldanhars nowadays whereas formerly they used to be his enemies — instead of acting in our favour, may be brewing mischief... If he is brewing mischief, would it be inconceivable for him with his wife and children, together with all the Watermen, to be taken to the Robben Island with sweet words and then left there so that we might trade more peaceably and satisfactorily with the natives of Saldanha, who appear to be a good sort of people? About all of this, time will show us more.

Extract from Van Riebeeck's diary.

Krotoa : Autshumato's niece

Pieter van Meerhoff, a Dutch settler, was the third Postholder on Robben Island. He was married to a Khoisan woman who grew up in Van Riebeeck's household. Her name was Krotoa and she was Autshumato's niece. She was the main translator for the Dutch before she accompanied her husband to Robben Island in 1655.

It must have been a lonely life on Robben Island for Krotoa, with no female friends. Soon after she arrived there, she began drinking heavily. Then her husband was sent to Madagascar on a slaving expedition and was killed.

So she returned to the mainland, hoping to find a place for herself in Dutch society. But she found that she was not accepted by the Dutch or by the Khoisan. Eventually her drinking and her behaviour became so unacceptable to the Dutch that she was banished to Robben Island as an outcast. She died there after eight lonely, isolated years.

Krotoa.

East Indian prisoners

By the mid-1600s more workers were needed to burn lime and cut stone on Robben Island, and to help produce fruit and vegetables for ships which were on their way to the East Indies.

Khoisan worked on the island and were paid in brandy and tobacco. Increasing numbers of convicts were imprisoned on the island to do hard labour, and some East Indian slaves were brought to work on the island. But as the 1600s came to a close, a new group of prisoners arrived on Robben Island – political opponents and leaders of resistance to Dutch rule in the East Indies. Among those banished to the island were people of noble birth and high rank.

The first eastern political prisoner on Robben Island arrived there in 1667. He was one of the *Orang Cayen* (Men of Power and Influence) of Sumatra. He was the first of many political exiles and convicts from the East who were imprisoned on the island. Many of these prisoners died on Robben Island after spending years in terrible prison conditions.

King Pangeran Chakra Deningrat, the King of Madura, spent at least 12 years imprisoned on the island before his death. He was imprisoned by the Dutch for encouraging the people of Madura, an island situated north-east of Java, to resist Dutch rule. Banished to Robben Island, he died there in 1754. Some people believe that his body is buried in the shrine on Robben Island, on the site where the Karamat is built.

The Robben Island Karamat – an Islamic shrine situated just outside the prison walls.

Muslim Karamats of the Cape

The Karamat of Sheik Yussuf on the Cape Flats, the Karamat of Hadje Matarim, and the graves of Muslim leaders on Robben Island, Signal Hill and in Groot Constantia and Simon's Town form a circle of Karamats. Muslim followers believe that these protect Cape Town from disasters such as earthquakes, fires and wars.

Others say that the Karamat is built over the grave of Hadje Matarim. Hadje Matarim was banished to the Cape in 1743, together with Tuan Sayed Alawie. Both men were Islamic priests and were probably sentenced to a life in chains on the island for spreading the teachings of Islam to slaves 'owned' by the Dutch. Hadje Matarim died after ten years on the island. Tuan Sayed Alawie was released after Hadje Matarim's death. He went on to become the first Imam of the Cape Muslim community.

There were many other exceptional men, kings, princes and religious leaders from the East who were banished to Robben Island. Unfortunately very little is known about them.

A page from the Bandieten Roll.

Prisoners on Robben Island were known as *bandieten* (bandits or convicts). The first Bandieten Roll (convict roll) dates from 1728. At this time there were 42 prisoners on the island – 26 Europeans and 16 *Indiaanen* (prisoners from the East Indies). The convicts lived in quarters known as 'Die Kraal', which were probably first used to house sheep. The prisoners' work was to collect shells and cut stone from the quarry.

A prison and a hospital

On 7 August 1795, British warships opened fire on the Dutch at Simon's Town and Muizenberg. The British Army moved onto the land, taking control of the Cape and ending 150 years of Dutch rule.

In the 1800s the British, like the Dutch before them, continued to use Robben Island as a prison. Prisoners included men who had deserted from the British Army; criminals convicted of crimes like theft, murder, assault and fraud; and political prisoners – local leaders who resisted British rule. But not all prisoners were on the island for criminal or political offences. From the mid-1800s the island was used more and more as a hospital for the extremely sick, the mentally ill (known as lunatics), the very poor, and the lepers.

Although a prison and a hospital are completely different institutions, they have one thing in common: both house the unwanted people of society. And Robben Island was a perfect dumping ground – where outcasts were 'out of sight and out of mind'.

Convicts carrying passengers and their cargo to a ship.

Robben Island: a political prison

The 1800s were marked by conflicts over land between the British and the Xhosa. The British Army forced the Xhosa across the Fish River into what is now Ciskei and Transkei, in a conflict known as the Hundred Years' War because it lasted one hundred years. Some Xhosa did not give up their land easily. They fought back in a series of battles now known as the Frontier Wars or Wars of Dispossession. Many of the Xhosa leaders captured by the British were sent to Robben Island. The Koranna people in the North fought similar battles and many of their leaders also became political prisoners on Robben Island.

These chiefs served their prison sentences in little huts at Murray's Bay on Robben Island. They were eventually moved to houses in 1863.

Makana.

Makana (Nxele)

Makana, also known as Nxele or Links, was a Xhosa warrior-prophet from the Eastern Cape. He led Xhosa armies against the British in the Frontier War of 1818–19. He said the ancestors and cattle would rise from the sea to help in the battle. But Makana underestimated the strength of the British weapons. He eventually surrendered to the British in an attempt to make peace for his starving people, and he was sent to Robben Island as a political prisoner.

In 1820, Makana and 30 other prisoners tried to escape from Robben Island. The boat carrying Makana capsized and he was drowned. But he became a lasting symbol of resistance. Still sometimes today Robben Island is called the Island of Makana.

Siyolo

Thirty years later Siyolo, a Ndlambe Xhosa chief, was captured by the British in the War of Mlangeni. He and his wife spent 14 years imprisoned on Robben Island before being released in 1869.

Nongqawuse.

Maqoma and other chiefs

In April 1856 a young girl called Nongqawuse said that her ancestors had spoken to her in a vision. Their message was that the Xhosa community would rise up from the dead and become strong again. But for this to happen, the people must slaughter all their cattle and stop planting crops. The Xhosa chief Sarhili ordered all his chiefs to obey. For a whole year cattle were slaughtered and crops were not planted, which nearly destroyed the Xhosa.

As part of a systematic campaign to destroy the independence of the Xhosa, Cape Governor, Sir George Grey, used the cattle killing to undermine the traditional authority of the chiefs. A number of chiefs were falsely accused of various offences and exiled.

The Ngqika chief, Maqoma, whose influence was most feared, was sentenced to 20 years on Robben Island. His wife Katyi was allowed to accompany him. Other chiefs imprisoned included Maqoma's half-brother Xhoxho, Mhala, Phato (of the Gqunukwebe line) and his son Dilima, Stokwe of the Mbalu Chiefdom, and Fadana. By the end of 1857 more than 900 Xhosa had been transported to Cape Town, some ending up on Robben Island and others in the Breakwater Prison on the Waterfront.

Maqoma was released in 1869. But two years later he was recaptured after he tried to reclaim his land. Once again he found himself a prisoner on Robben Island, this time without his wife. He died two years later in 1873.

Maqoma.

Langalibalele

In the late 1800s the British said that all African people must register their weapons with the authorities. The Hlubi refused to do this. So the British sent troops after Langalibalele, the Hlubi chief. He escaped into the mountains of Lesotho. But he was finally arrested and unfairly convicted of treason, murder and rebellion. He was sent to Robben Island with his son. He spent a year on the island before being allowed to return to Natal in 1887. He died two years later.

The Gcaleka

In 1877, war broke out between the Gcaleka (a Xhosa clan) and the Mfengu (a group of refugees who had British support). This led to the ninth and final Frontier War, where the Xhosa were crushed. After this war, 11 Gcaleka Xhosa and the sons of Maqoma, Mhala and Sandile were imprisoned on Robben Island.

Sandile.

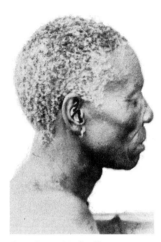

Stockwe Tyhali.

Stockwe Tyhali

Stockwe Tyhali was a chief from Thembuland. He was charged with high treason and sentenced to life imprisonment on Robben Island. However, he was released in 1883.

The Koranna

On the Northern Frontier, a group called the Koranna also resisted British rule in a series of wars. After the first Koranna War, leaders like Piet Rooy, David Diedericks, Jan Kivido and Carel Ruyter were sent to Robben Island. Kivido died soon after he arrived on the island, and the other three were released after 14 years' imprisonment.

Many more leaders were captured and imprisoned on Robben Island after the second Koranna War. Some leaders were removed from the island and sent to the Breakwater Prison. The remaining leaders on Robben Island refused the British Government's offer of conditional release.

As the 1800s drew to an end, the political prison on Robben Island was closed. It took much longer for the hospital section to close its doors and move all the patients off this lonely place of exile.

In the mid-1800s many ordinary criminals were moved from Robben Island and were set to work building roads on the mainland. Many mountain passes, like Sir Lowry's Pass and Chapman's Peak Drive, were built by these prisoners.

Robben Island: a hospital

Patients in the Robben Island hospital during the 1800s lived like the prisoners before them – in terrible conditions. No-one tried to treat or cure them. In fact, patients received the same cruel treatment as dangerous criminals. Patients complained that they were chained and beaten; they were seldom allowed any visitors; patients assaulted each other; and there were cases of male lunatics raping the extremely sick women patients. The lepers complained about the island itself – they said that it was moist, damp and unwholesome. There was a constant glare from the surrounding water, and they felt that it was a place of sorrow, horror and lonely exile. One patient said that the only excitement to be had on the barren island was tobacco smoking.

Male lunatic patient.

The lunatics

'Lunatics' was the name used in the 1800s for the mentally insane, but it also included hobos, prostitutes and some criminals. Some lunatics were placed on Robben Island by the courts, others were sent by their families, and some even came on their own.

At first all patients lived together in the old prison buildings, sheds and stables. Then, in the mid-1800s, the lunatics were separated from the other patients. Black lunatics mainly lived in the 'Kraal' – which in previous centuries had been used for sheep and later for the East Indian prisoners. White lunatics lived in a building called the 'Asylum'. In 1921 all the lunatics were removed from the island.

Plaatjies was one of the lunatics who was sent to Robben Island. He had one aim in life – to reach the mainland. Over and over again he built his own boats out of box-wood and made his own coins of brass to spend on the mainland. As he finished building one boat, the authorities would destroy it. But he never lost hope, and would simply start again. Plaatjies never reached the mainland.

The extremely sick

The first patients on Robben Island were mainly sailors and soldiers who had no money and were too sick or too old to work. There were also some ex-slaves who could not support themselves, and women who had been prostitutes or who had sexually transmitted diseases. Some patients were alcoholics. All these patients were expected to look after each other, and they received no treatment. Most patients had left the island by 1891.

The lepers

Until the 1940s there was no known cure for leprosy. Doctors did not know how people got leprosy or how it was passed from one person to another. People were afraid that leprosy was very contagious. By the 1840s people wanted lepers off the mainland and out of sight. But it was really only in the 1890s that the number of lepers on Robben Island increased, after the government passed the Leprosy Suppression Act. This Act said that lepers must live completely apart from the rest of society, in hospitals or at home. 'Lepers flocked to Robben Island. They came with hopes of cures, by force and in fear of persecution by a nervous public ...' (Harriet Deacon, in *Robben Island: The Politics of Rock and Sand* University of Cape Town)

Female lepers in 1915.

A leper colony

In the 1890s lepers lived apart from other patients on Robben Island for the first time. They were placed in 'hokkies' or 'pondocks', which were old chicken sheds. In 1892 Franz Jacobs led the lepers in a rebellion about their conditions. Jacobs wrote a letter to the Queen of England saying that lepers were treated like prisoners. The rebellion was broken when extra men were brought over from the mainland as leper police. Jacobs was removed from the island and placed at the Old Somerset Hospital until he repented. But there was a small victory – the following year the government allowed families of lepers free passes to Robben Island to visit the lepers and paid for the postage of their parcels.

By the beginning of the 1900s conditions for lepers had improved. All buildings were repaired and painted. A new block was built for male lepers. Bathrooms and toilets were also built, and recreation was introduced.

Resistance to this cruel separation of lepers from the rest of society continued until the 1930s. At that time all lepers were moved from the island and placed in hospitals on the mainland. Robben Island had become a well-established town. It had a dairy, piggery, schools, fire department, bakery, parks, library, recreation halls, police force, mule-drawn tram, and churches. Before the lepers left there were about 2 000 people on the island, including patients and staff. When the last lepers were moved, all buildings used by the lepers were destroyed and the island was left in the hands of the lighthouse-keepers and a few workers.

The last patients from Robben Island leave Cape Town harbour on their way to a hospital near Pretoria.

Robben Island For Sale

On April 1, 1930, Robben Island will be available to whoever makes the most attractive offer for it to the Lands Department.

It was officially stated yesterday that the leper colony, and everything on the island that has been in contact with leprosy, will be burned down. On March 31 all patients will be taken off the island to a better hospital near Pretoria. The only people who will remain on the island will be the lighthouse-keepers and their families.

The authorities stated yesterday, "No effort will be spared to demolish the leper buildings. The island will be ready for any use that may be decided upon, after it has been evacuated by the last patient."

Village will be left

The leper buildings will be burnt immediately. Many of the buildings are made of wood and iron, and are old and dilapidated. But the village will be left alone. It has hundreds of trees, gardens and could house about 2 000 people. There is a telephone cable from the mainland, several boreholes, and a number of windmills. There are roads, a bioscope and a landing jetty.

Suggested uses

The Cape Times suggested some uses for the island:

- First prize in a State lottery
- A reformatory
- A government farm colony for alcoholics
- A home for orphans
- A health resort
- A training ground for the Defence Force
- A municipal amusement park.

Anyone wanting to buy the island must apply to the Secretary for Lands.

In the meantime the future of the island is undecided.

From *The Cape Times*.

The first step towards the final evacuation of all lepers from Robben Island – the white lepers' quarters going up in flames.

Robben Island: a military base

In 1936, shortly before the Second World War, the Defence Force took over Robben Island. They saw the island as a key point in the defence of Cape Town. At that time there was no harbour, no supply of fresh water and no electricity on the island. The roads badly needed to be repaired and there were not enough buildings to house soldiers.

Gun turret on Robben Island.

Within months the Defence Force turned the island into a heavily defended military base with the most up-to-date weapons and military installations in the country at that time.

In the 1940s a training camp for 'coloured' soldiers was set up on the island. Within a few weeks of opening the camp, several hundred men had been trained. Women from the Coastal Artillery were also posted to Robben Island.

Robben Island was on the war maps

By Tom Jessop
At the beginning of the Second World War men and materials were rushed from the mainland to Robben Island so that Cape Town would be defended in case of enemy attack.

"The island then was just a pile of rubbish – there wasn't even a supply of fresh water," said Brigadier Craig. "We decided to anticipate Dunkirk. We grabbed every fishing boat we could find and moved 150 000 tons of materials across from the mainland to the island. We even had to take sand to make concrete, as the sand of the island was unsuitable. It was a grim night-and-day race against time.

The war office set us a 23-month programme, but we finished the job in four months, including the building of the gun emplacements, an underground power station and the other installations."

Sergeant-Major Oosthuizen took up the tale where Brigadier Craig had left off. It had been Oosthuizen's task to position the guns on the island.

He told me that there was a delay in getting gun parts from Britain and so dummy guns were placed on the island "to deceive any enemy agent who might become a little too curious."

The first gun arrived in 1941. The task of off-loading and mounting the guns was not an easy one. There was no harbour and there were no cranes to off-load the gun parts.

Adapted from *The Cape Times*, 9 August 1947.

But transport to and from the island was always a problem. Soldiers and equipment were transported by hired fishing boats and the trip could take up to three hours, depending upon the sea and the boat's engine.

By the end of the Second World War the island had completely changed. There was a fully equipped arms-store 18 m under the ground. There were workshops, enough water, good roads, a harbour, a landing strip for aircraft, and sports and recreation facilities. There were new bungalows, messes and wash-houses. A new power-station was working and provided electricity. There were rows of modern houses. A new boat was bought so that the crossing could be done in 45 to 50 minutes, and the airport was working. Three thousand people lived on the island in relative comfort.

Robben Island was described as: 'the deluxe military station of South Africa, with comfortable living quarters and messes, ample recreational facilities, including two concert halls, which might better be described as theatres, several billiard rooms, tennis courts, football fields, and everything designed to make the soldier's life a happy one.' (W. Henry, *The Cape Times*, 2 February 1946)

In the 1950s Robben Island was taken over by the South African Navy and used as a training centre. Between 20 and 30 families lived permanently on the island until it was taken over by the Prisons Department.

In the 1940s a training camp for coloured soldiers was set up on Robben Island.

SECTION 2
Robben Island: apartheid's prison

Apartheid rule

Segregation and discrimination started in South Africa long before the National Party came to power in 1948. But from that year onwards, South Africa entered its darkest period ever, as the policy of apartheid was enforced throughout the country.

Almost immediately the new government passed discriminatory laws to control every aspect of black peoples' lives: laws about where people could live, work, trade, go to school, the type of schooling they could receive, who they could marry, and who they could have sexual relations with. The government and its security forces also took extreme measures to crush resistance to these laws.

Leaders and members of liberation movements were arrested and banished, while others went into hiding or exile. Opposition movements and organisations were banned. Over the following years, thousands of people sacrificed their lives and their freedom, fighting these unjust laws. But the people were not silenced.

Sharpeville 1960: 69 people were killed and 186 wounded at a peaceful demonstration against the pass laws. The government's reaction to the spread of non-violent protest was to declare a state of emergency. More than 11 000 people were arrested, and the ANC and PAC were banned.

With the increasing state violence, opposition organisations were faced with a choice:

> *The people's patience is not endless. The time comes in the life of any nation when there remain only two choices: submit or fight. That time has now come in South Africa.* (From the Manifesto of Umkhonto we Sizwe, 1961)

At the same time as the ANC adopted a policy of armed struggle, it appealed to the international community to help in the struggle against apartheid:

> *We shall ask all our millions of friends outside South Africa to intensify the boycott and isolation of the government of this country, diplomatically, economically, and in every other way.* (From an article by Nelson Mandela published by the underground ANC in South Africa and its offices abroad, June 1961)

On 16 December 1961 Umkhonto we Sizwe announced its existence with a series of explosions throughout the country. At the end of 1961, Poqo – the armed wing of the PAC – was formed. Due to the emergence of these resistance armies, the government passed the first detention-without-trial laws in 1963. Both the PAC and ANC were hard hit; 3 246 Poqo members were detained. Of these, 124 were convicted of murder and 46 were hanged.

In 1962 Nelson Mandela returned from a tour of African states, seeking support for the armed struggle, and was arrested. Nearly a year later, police surrounded an old farmhouse in Rivonia, outside Johannesburg. They had received a tip-off that several leaders of the Congress Alliance were staying there. Sisulu, Goldberg, Mbeki, Kathrada and others were arrested and later charged with sabotage.

The Rivonia Trial (1963–1964) resulted in the high command of Umkhonto we Sizwe being convicted and sentenced to life imprisonment. Seven of these trialists were to serve their sentences on Robben Island, which had become a fully segregated prison reserved for black male prisoners.

Once again this island became a place of banishment and exile, and once again it became a symbol of people's resistance.

The 1973 Durban strikes.

Detentions, bannings, arrests and political trials during the 1960s crippled the resistance movements. But the 1970s saw a renewed wave of mass action. Black workers in an increasingly powerful trade union movement organised rolling strike action throughout the country. A new political direction and leadership emerged in the form of the Black Consciousness Movement (BCM). SASO (the South African Students' Organisation) was founded in 1969 under Steve Biko, and students and youth began organising themselves at universities, colleges and schools.

There were also changes outside South Africa which gave new hope to those resisting apartheid – the fighting in Namibia and Zimbabwe and the collapse of Portuguese rule in Mozambique and Angola. Foreign governments began imposing sanctions, businesses started disinvesting from South Africa, and international grassroots organisations began mass protests and campaigns. The ANC set up offices throughout Europe and bases in neighbouring countries such as Lesotho and Zambia.

On 16 June 1976 secondary school children marched in Soweto in protest against the use of Afrikaans. Hundreds of people were killed in the violence that followed, as the uprising spread to every major city, village and homeland throughout South Africa.

Thousands of young people fled the country to join the liberation struggle. A massive state clampdown followed the Soweto uprising, and a new wave of political prisoners flooded South African jails. A new section was built on Robben Island to hold people sentenced after the 1976 uprising, as the armed struggle resulted in many more young men being imprisoned on the island.

The 1980s saw an increasing unity amongst many of the important forces for change in South Africa:

> *The degree of unity attained is almost unprecedented anywhere in the country at any time in its history. A base has been created upon which lasting buildings of the future can be erected.*
> (From a pamphlet distributed during the 1980s school boycotts, quoted in *The Right to Learn*, published by SACHED Books)

This new unity paved the way for the formation of two mass-based umbrella organisations in 1983 – the National Forum and the United Democratic Front. At the same time the armed struggle intensified as the ANC called on the people of South Africa to make the country ungovernable.

Repression intensified too, and in July 1985 the government declared the first state of emergency, giving its security forces enormous powers to crush resistance. Once again, organisations were banned and thousands of people were detained without trial, including hundreds of children under 16.

'... in the many incidents that filled those crowded days that followed the first shootings of 16 June 1976, the youth were able to show South Africa and the world that there was the will and determination to end the apartheid system.' (B. Hirson, *Year of Fire, Year of Ash*, **Zed Press**)

School boycotts reached a peak in the 1980s.

COSATU House was bombed, and many trade unionists were detained and harassed. International protest caused the government to lift the state of emergency in March 1986, but it was reinstated three months later and renewed in June 1987.

By the late 1980s, despite the government's extreme measures, much of the country was 'ungovernable'. The labour movements were showing their power through consumer boycotts and 'living wage' campaigns which seriously threatened the country's economy, and international pressure and sanctions were taking their toll on every sector of South African society.

In 1986 Nelson Mandela initiated the first talks with the South African government around a negotiated settlement, thus paving the way for the first democratic elections in South Africa in 1994.

Mandela's 70th birthday in 1988 provided the focus for a massive international campaign aimed at releasing all political prisoners in South Africa.

Mandela was finally released unconditionally in February 1990.

During the 1980s Mandela himself was offered conditional release on several occasions, provided that he would denounce the ANC's armed struggle. He refused these offers: 'I am not prepared to sell the birthright of the people to be free ... Your freedom and mine cannot be separated. I will return.'

Strengthened by the growing resistance to apartheid by the South African people, political prisoners on Robben Island waged powerful struggles of their own.

Welcome to Robben Island!

The entrance to the prison.

The Department of Prisons took over Robben Island from the South African Navy in April 1961. Within a short time the Department began transporting political prisoners to the island. Its task was to crush the spirit of these opponents of apartheid and to break their morale.

When we arrived at Cape Town harbour the truck pulled in right next to a little passenger boat called Diaz. Still handcuffed and chained we were taken aboard and placed in a hold below the deck. Many of the prisoners had never seen the sea before, let alone been on a boat ... We could see the sea splashing outside, a little bit rough, and the boat rolled from one side to the other. It was frightening for many of the prisoners. Going through their minds over and over again was the question: What is Robben Island like, that dreaded prison we have heard so much about? What is the island really like? Indres Naidoo of the ANC, sentenced to ten years on Robben Island

The Robbe

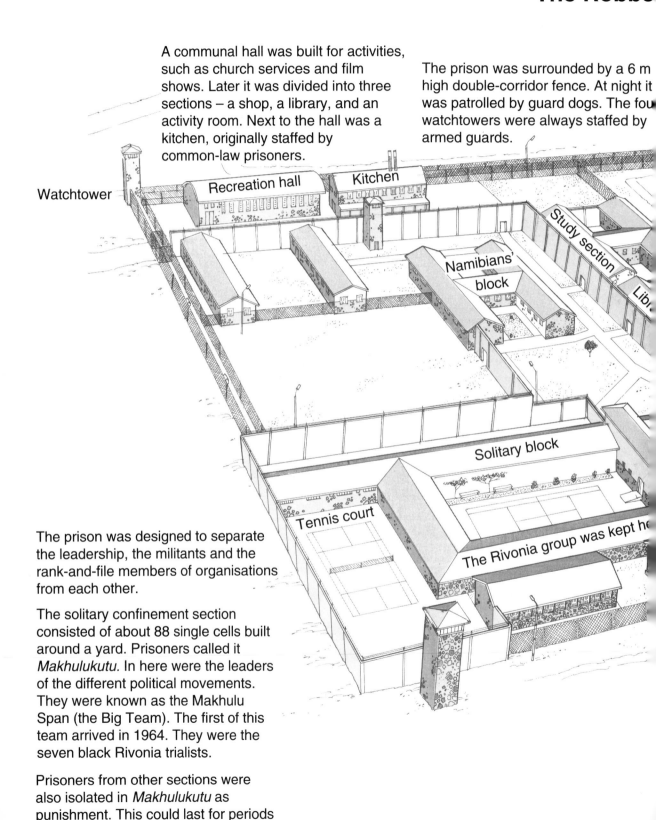

A communal hall was built for activities, such as church services and film shows. Later it was divided into three sections – a shop, a library, and an activity room. Next to the hall was a kitchen, originally staffed by common-law prisoners.

The prison was surrounded by a 6 m high double-corridor fence. At night it was patrolled by guard dogs. The fou watchtowers were always staffed by armed guards.

Watchtower

Recreation hall

Kitchen

Study section

Namibians' block

Libr

Solitary block

Tennis court

The Rivonia group was kept he

The prison was designed to separate the leadership, the militants and the rank-and-file members of organisations from each other.

The solitary confinement section consisted of about 88 single cells built around a yard. Prisoners called it *Makhulukutu.* In here were the leaders of the different political movements. They were known as the Makhulu Span (the Big Team). The first of this team arrived in 1964. They were the seven black Rivonia trialists.

Prisoners from other sections were also isolated in *Makhulukutu* as punishment. This could last for periods of one day to six months or longer.

This drawing was developed from a s

...land Prison

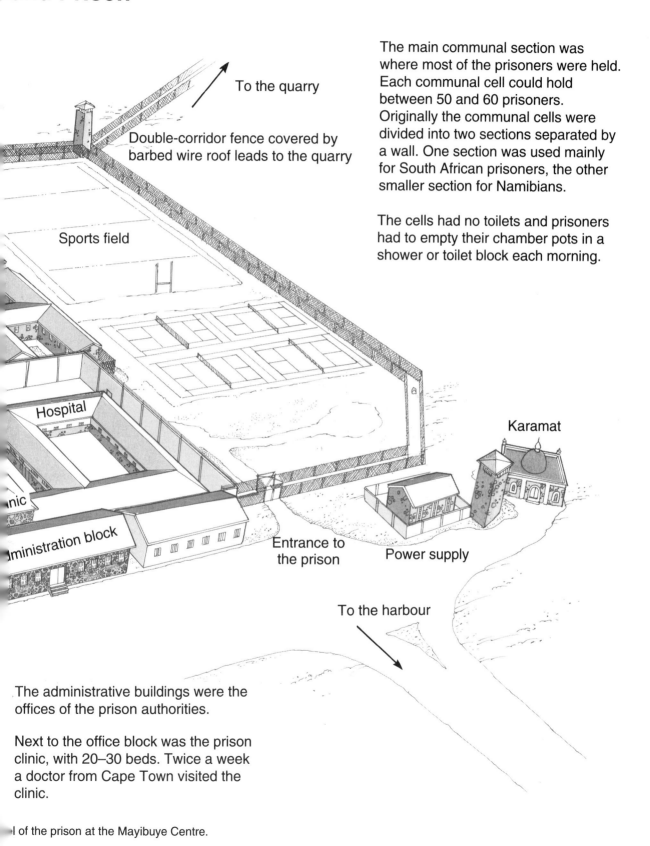

To the quarry

Double-corridor fence covered by
barbed wire roof leads to the quarry

Sports field

Hospital

...nic

...dministration block

Entrance to
the prison

Power supply

Karamat

To the harbour

The main communal section was
where most of the prisoners were held.
Each communal cell could hold
between 50 and 60 prisoners.
Originally the communal cells were
divided into two sections separated by
a wall. One section was used mainly
for South African prisoners, the other
smaller section for Namibians.

The cells had no toilets and prisoners
had to empty their chamber pots in a
shower or toilet block each morning.

The administrative buildings were the
offices of the prison authorities.

Next to the office block was the prison
clinic, with 20–30 beds. Twice a week
a doctor from Cape Town visited the
clinic.

...l of the prison at the Mayibuye Centre.

Prisoners of the island

In 1978 it was announced in Parliament that there were 440 convicted political prisoners in South Africa. These prisoners were from different liberation movements, but most were members of the ANC and PAC. Four hundred of the 440 were on Robben Island. The rest were in Kroonstad and Pretoria Local Prison. At least 54 of the Robben Island prisoners were Namibians, 20 sentenced to life imprisonment. There were also 20 South Africans who had been sentenced to life imprisonment. At this time there were also at least six Robben Island prisoners who were under the age of 16 and serving five-year sentences.

Common-law prisoners and political prisoners

In the early 1960s common-law prisoners and political prisoners could mix freely. Common-law prisoners helped political prisoners smuggle news in and out of jail.

Then in 1971 the authorities decided to house political prisoners and common-law prisoners separately. From then on there was a wall of censorship around political prisoners: they were not allowed to receive any news; their visits were closely supervised; their prison sentences could not be changed; studying was severely restricted; and these prisoners were almost always served with banning or banishment orders on leaving prison.

> *In the early years, before the segregation of common-law prisoners from political prisoners, the source of newspapers was the common-law prisoners ... they could smuggle any contraband stuff into gaol, including newspapers.*

> *Although the original idea of mixing political prisoners and common-law prisoners appeared to have been to harass and humiliate the politicos, the idea boomeranged in the end. Instead, the political prisoners quickly assumed a position of influence and dominance, to the extent that the common-law prisoners were soon at the beck and call of their political fellow inmates.*
> Michael Dingake of the ANC, sentenced to 15 years on Robben Island

---

Tsafendas

In 1966 Dr Verwoerd, leader of the National Party, was assassinated. His assassin, Dimitrio Tsafendas, was brought to Robben Island and held in *Makhulukutu*. His cell was walled off from the other cells so that he could have no contact at all with the other prisoners. He was later transferred from Robben Island to an unknown destination.

The Rivonia trialists – ANC

Nelson Mandela, Govan Mbeki, Walter Sisulu, Ahmed Kathrada, Dennis Goldberg, Lionel Bernstein, Raymond Mhlaba, Andrew Mlangeni, Elias Motsoaledi and others, all of the ANC, were tried in the Pretoria Supreme Court from October 1963 to June 1964.

During my lifetime I have dedicated myself to the struggle of the African people. I have cherished the ideal of a democratic and free society ... it is an ideal which I hope to live for and to achieve. But, if needs be, it is an ideal for which I am prepared to die. Nelson Mandela during the Rivonia Trial

Nelson Mandela (left), Ahmed Kathrada (centre) and Walter Sisulu (right).

Robert Sobukwe

A house stood completely on its own, fenced in and guarded by an armed warder. In the doorway we could see the figure of Robert Sobukwe, leader of the PAC, dressed in civilian clothing. The PAC chaps with us were very excited to be near their leader ... It was clear that he was in no position to greet us, nor could we greet him in anyway. But he managed every now and then to move his head in such a way as to show he had recognised us as political prisoners... Indres Naidoo

Robert Sobukwe.

In 1963 Robert Sobukwe completed his three-year prison sentence.

He was immediately detained on Robben Island for another six years under a special law called the 'Sobukwe clause'. He was held in a 'cottage' outside the main prison, completely on his own. Only his wife was allowed to visit him occasionally and stay in the cottage. Later, Sobukwe was removed from Robben Island and taken to the mainland. He died while still under house arrest.

The 'Sobukwe clause' was used as psychological torture against political prisoners with short-term sentences. Under this law, anybody could be detained indefinitely after completing a prison sentence imposed by the Courts.

Jeff Masemola

A member of the PAC, Jeff Masemola was charged in 1963 with conspiracy to commit sabotage, along with 14 others. Masemola was sentenced to life imprisonment on Robben Island.

Herman Toivo ja Toivo.

Andimba Herman Toivo ja Toivo

Herman Toivo ja Toivo, leader of SWAPO, was charged alongside Shityuwete, Shiponeni, Tjipahura, Tshaningau and others under the Terrorism Act in mid-1967 and tried in the Pretoria Terrorism Trial, September 1967 to February 1968. He was sentenced to 20 years' imprisonment on Robben Island.

SASO/BPC Trialists

Cooper, Cindi, Lekota, Mokoape, Moodley, Myeza, Nefolov-Hodwe, Nkomo and Sedibe were tried in the SASO/BPC trial in the Pretoria Supreme Court from June 1975 to December 1976, on charges under the Terrorism Act.

The struggle for survival

Life as a prisoner was a constant fight for survival. Soon after arriving on the island, political prisoners organised themselves for this fight. Their solidarity, discipline and courage kept them alive. Together, they fought for their rights to decent food, humane work, fair and just treatment, decent living conditions, information, education and recreation.

Nelson Mandela and Walter Sisulu in the prison yard on Robben Island.

The right to fair and just treatment

In the early 1960s the authorities removed all coloured warders from Robben Island. Some of these warders had been sympathetic to political prisoners and had helped to smuggle in tobacco, newspapers, letters and radios – anything to give comfort to the prisoners.

By 1963 Robben Island became a maximum security prison, where all warders were white, and all prisoners were black – either African, coloured or Indian. Most of the warders were from poor working-class backgrounds. They were so indoctrinated that they actually believed that black people were animals, not human beings, and that black political prisoners were hardened criminals. Warders were abusive and quick to punish.

Assaults

In the first few years on the island warders treated prisoners particularly cruelly. Ex-prisoners still remember 28 May 1971 for the brutal raid in which prisoners were beaten, stripped and searched. This happened after all prisoners went on a hunger strike in sympathy with Namibian prisoners.

> *Armed with batons, they raided our single cells in batches of three and four. 'Teen die muur!' (Against the wall!) 'Trek uit.' (Strip.) A number of prisoners in the segregation section were assaulted. They had their balls twisted, they were punched and kicked. Andimba Toivo ja Toivo, the SWAPO leader, was one of those who was severely beaten. After the assault, like the other victims of that 28th day of May 1971, he was forced to clean his blood-spattered cell.* Michael Dingake

> *Prisoners were ordered to run around inside the yard of the zinc jail. To run fast, touching the four corners of the yard. The warders lined up, batons in hand. They were raw Boers determined to unleash their raw hatred on the Poqos ... They lashed out at the panting prisoners. They lashed out with the heavy batons screaming: Where is Leballo now? Where is Sobukwe? Where is Nkrumah? They lashed indiscriminately – on the head, ribs, shoulders, buttocks, stomach and arms. Every time the baton landed, it landed with a sickening sound.*
> DM Zwelonke (PAC)

All prisoners on the same island

While warders were from poor white families, the leaders of prisoners were mainly from black, middle-class, educated backgrounds:

> *... given the racist situation in South Africa, it was an act of unimaginable cruelty to place poor white, unemployable male warders in charge of, in most cases, extremely sensitive, basically*

*law-abiding, black prisoners with aspirations towards human
rights and freedom. It was an act of unimaginable cruelty both to
us and to them.* Neville Alexander, sentenced to 10 years on
Robben Island

So prisoners and warders came from completely different
backgrounds. But both were, in a sense, imprisoned on the same
island.

*Conditions for the warders were not good. They could leave the
island for only three days a fortnight, and then only with written
permission. There was very little recreation for them ... Seventy-
five per cent or more were bachelors and the only female company
they could look forward to was the wives of the other twenty-five
per cent, and their infant daughters – young girls escaped from
the island as soon as they could.* Indres Naidoo

**Armed warder on
launch leaving the
island.**

Prisoners learnt to forgive, but did not forget, as Neville Alexander
explains:

*The political maturity reached by most of us in prison is the
reason for the lack of bitterness which people always comment*

upon when they speak to ex-Robben Island prisoners ... many of us understood better than the warders why they acted the way they did; we could explain to them sometimes why it was that they acted the way they did ... Most of us felt strongly that it was important to forgive, not to forget.

This is what Eastern Cape advocate Fikele Bam had to say about warders, on his return to Robben Island in 1994, 20 years after he was imprisoned there:

Not all warders were bad. We discovered and so did they, that they had a humanity, they discovered we had a humanity.
(As quoted in *Democracy in Action*, IDASA, May 1994.)

As well as learning about the humanity that they shared with their prisoners, warders also learnt other things. The prisoners became the teachers in an ironic reversal of roles. They tutored the warders in subjects such as Maths, English, History and even Home Economics, and in this way assisted warders in furthering their education and careers.

The authorities soon realised that they could not keep one set of warders on the island for too long, as warders were being influenced by prisoners. So every two or three years warders were replaced, and then the education would begin again.

Walter Sisulu with his former warder, Luyanda Ka Msumza who is now with the Quaker Peace Centre.

Organisation, discipline, courage

The prison is above all punitive, it operates to break the human spirit, to exploit human weakness, undermine human strength, destroy initiative, individuality, negate intelligence and process an amorphous, robot-like mass. The great challenge is how to resist, how not to adjust, to keep intact the knowledge of society outside and to live by its rules, for that is the only way to maintain the human and social within you ...

In the course of time, we established our committees: disciplinary, educational, political, recreational, literary, and these helped to ensure that we shared the meagre facilities available to us equitably. The authorities came to recognise, unofficially of course, that, in the final analysis, order in the prison was preserved, not by the warders, but by ourselves.
Nelson Mandela (ANC), sentenced to life imprisonment

Prisoners fought back. Organisations survived, with structures and with an identifiable leadership. They formed committees for day-to-day administration, for organisational discipline, for developing a study programme, for organising recreational activities, and for opening communication channels between different sections. Through these committees prisoners could respond to their harsh conditions in an organised and disciplined way.

Hunger strikes

Hunger strikes were a powerful weapon used by prisoners to change conditions. Through such protest, prisoners won some privileges and victories. This kind of organised, disciplined and courageous action kept prisoners alive and sane.

Even though the prison authorities tried to isolate prisoners from each other, they quickly established an underground network. Hunger strikes took place over and over again in all sections. A strike would start in one section in the morning, and by afternoon all the sections were on hunger strike.

The hunger strike had started in the communal cells in protest against the poor and inadequate prison rations and for improvement of general prison conditions. Communication lines with the segregation section were officially non-existent but unofficially alive, though a bit slow, underground. The segregation section learned of the strike a day after and joined in sympathy. Michael Dingake

Protesters supporting hunger strikers on the island.

Despite the attempts of the prison authorities to play off one section against the other by false reports, the solidarity between prisoners of different sections was never broken.

The right to humane work

Most prisoners were sentenced to hard labour. Before 1970 this meant:
* working in either the stone or lime quarries;
* collecting seaweed in the ice-cold sea; and
* various other work such as building roads, clearing fields and chopping wood.

The stone quarries

Until the 1970s, most political prisoners from the communal cells worked in the stone quarries. There were two quarries of bluestone right on the beach, and a limestone quarry in the centre of the island.

It was hard work at the stone quarry. Compressor drills vibrated the whole day, shaking their operators like reeds in the wind. Some prisoners wielded huge hammers and pounded metal pins with all their might to split huge rocks embedded below sea level. The bulk of prisoners sat in arranged groups to break the rock pieces into smaller pieces. Each prisoner had a daily standard quota to fulfil. Failure to fulfil the quota was punishable. The rest of the workspan carted the crushed stones around in wheelbarrows. Blisters and callused hands were the hallmarks of quarry span prisoners. Michael Dingake

The lime quarry

In 1965 the men in the single cells were taken to work in the lime quarry. Here they had to dig limestone with a pick and shovel, cut it and load it onto trucks. They worked in this quarry for about eight or nine years.

The island has got terrible extremes of climate. It can be blistering hot in summer, and even more punishing in the lime quarry. The reflection from the lime catches the sunlight and throws it back on to you and it can be extremely sharp and scorching. In winter it can become bitterly cold, raining or drizzling most of the time, with gusty winds. Mac Maharaj (ANC), sentenced to 12 years' imprisonment on Robben Island

... we were sent to work in the two lime quarries, chipping away at the rock-face with only picks, shovels and spades. It was very hard work, and a dazzling glare came off the white rocks when the sun shone – as we had no sunglasses, the eyesight of many of us was damaged. Helao Shityuwete (SWAPO), sentenced to 16 years on Robben Island

The prison authorities promised the Red Cross that they would stop the lime work. But despite their promises, they only stopped

Nelson Mandela in 1994, standing in the limestone quarry where he swung a pickaxe for many years.

it around 1975. In the meantime, alongside the breaking-up, shovelling and loading of lime, prisoners organised a programme of 'study classes'. As Michael Dingake says: 'The lime quarry was, even at the worst of times, a site for intellectual stimulation.'

Seaweed collection

In the early years the single-cell prisoners also sometimes had to collect seaweed. This involved standing knee-deep in the cold sea water and collecting the seaweed with their bare hands. In winter this work was very painful. But they caught other things too:

> *The water was very clear and the crayfish were plentiful on the side of the island where the sewage pipe was. We would search them out among the rocks and then braai them on drums on the beach – the warders we would reward with some.* Nelson Mandela in *The Cape Times*, 12 February 1994

Workshops

Statue made by prisoners.

By the late 1970s the rock quarries were no longer in use, as they were flooded. New workshops were built which included facilities for more creative work, which the prisoners had demanded. In these workshops prisoners did carpentry, brick-making, brick-laying, plastering, upholstering, tailoring and shoe-making.

The fight for decent conditions

A favourite question from visitors to Robben Island was the food question: 'What sort of food do they give you?'

Our food was poor and unappetising. But the major grievance against the prison diet was that it was discriminatory. Coloured and Indian prisoners had one diet and Africans another.
Michael Dingake

Breakfast was a plate of porridge with one spoon of sugar if we were African ('F diet') and two spoons of sugar if we were coloured or Indian ('D diet'). We also got a cup of artificial soup and a cup of dreadful black coffee – no milk.

For lunch 'D diets' got a plate of mielie rice, and three times a week, either dried peas or beans. African prisoners got almost the same, but they also got a cup of phusamandla *– a powdered drink made from corn.*

In the evenings the 'D diets' were supposed to receive a quarter of a loaf of bread and eight ounces of vegetables, a cup of black coffee, a cup of the soup. Four days a week, we were to get four ounces of meat. In reality, we rarely got the vegetables. Instead of bread, the African comrades got a plate of porridge, and only two ounces of meat. But they were lucky to get even half of their ration of meat, so great was the smuggling by the common-law prisoners who prepared the food. This is how it was, apartheid inside apartheid, down to the tiniest details, even in the heart of the prison.
Indres Naidoo

In 1979 we were told that a non-racial diet had been approved in principle by the policy-makers. But they were not sure when it would be implemented. When we complained about the slowness of the process, we were advised, 'have patience' for the dietician was busy, very busy. Michael Dingake

'Apartheid within apartheid' – the prison menu reflected the policy of segregation in the prison. (Adapted from a table in Michael Dingake *My Fight Against Apartheid*)

Item	Coloureds/Asians	Africans
Mealie meal/ mealie rice/samp	400 g	350 g
Mealies	–	250 g
Bread	250 g	–
Meat or fish	110 g (4 x weekly)	60 g (4 x weekly)
Dried beans	125 g (meatless days)	125 g (meatless days)
Vegetables	250 g	250 g
Soup/Protone/ gravy powder	20 g	20 g
Fat	30 g	15 g
Milk	–	–
Coffee or tea	Twice daily	Once daily
Phusamandla	–	55 g
Salt	15 g	15 g
Sugar	60 g	45 g

The cells

We were locked up with a sanitary bucket, a bottle, a towel, a face cloth, three sleeping mats (one grass and two felt) and four blankets. That meagre space and those few belongings constituted our world for six weeks. We were let out of it for an hour each day: in the morning to shower and use the toilets, and in the afternoon to breathe fresh air and stretch our limbs. Strini Moodley (SASO), sentenced to five years' imprisonment on Robben Island

Nelson Mandela, like all the other prisoners in the single cells, lived in a concrete cell the size of a small room. At first he was only given a bed roll and a grass mat, and no other furniture – no bench, no table, no bed. After protests from prisoners in the single cells, they were all given small tables, and later benches and a wooden shelf. Some prisoners made their own cupboards from cardboard, paper and plastic. In about 1973 Nelson Mandela slept in a bed for the first time in ten years as he was ill; and he was given a chair instead of a bench, because he had back problems. By the late 1970s there were only 13 prisoners on the whole island who had beds.

Nelson Mandela's cell.

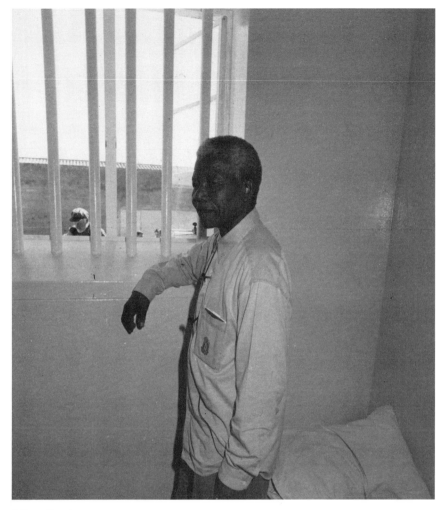

Mandela revisits his
old prison cell in 1994.

Blankets

*We started off by only being allowed two blankets, then we
demanded more and were given slim increases, one by one, till
today blankets are adequate, a minimum of five. No bedding in
the form of bedsheets, pillows, bedspreads, or pyjamas is provided
for black political prisoners.* Mac Maharaj, 1978

Clothing

*This used to be made out of khaki and sailcloth, with one thin
jersey given to you on 25 April and taken away on 25 September
irrespective of whether it was going to be hot or cold in the*

intervening period. You were given short pants, with Indians and coloureds allowed long pants in winter. But these things have changed, they've given us a warmer type of cloth for our jackets, they've given us long trousers which they now allow us to wear at any time of the year, African, Asian and coloured.
Mac Maharaj, 1978

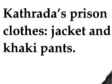

Kathrada's prison clothes: jacket and khaki pants.

A jersey knitted by James Maake, who was released in 1991.

Prison shoes 'comfort-fitted' by prisoners for the cold winters on Robben Island.

A few comforts

With dust everywhere and the chronic colds we all suffered, we had to wash out our hankies practically every day. At times they could be seen hanging out to dry, patches of coarse bright red material lodged between the bars of every cell, rows and rows of them stretching throughout the prison. The authorities accused us of flying the Red Flag and recalled every one of the red hankies. They gave us soft khaki ones instead, and at last we could blow our noses in peace. Indres Naidoo

Kathrada's fork, spoon, stainless steel milkpot and bowl.

A tea-strainer made specially for Ahmed Kathrada by Elias Motsoaledi.

A typical day in prison

From 1961, Robben Island was out of bounds to the general public and the Press. Then in 1977, the Department of Prisons decided to conduct a tour of the island for the Press.

Mac Maharaj comments on the newspaper articles that appeared in 1977: ... *(they) certainly saw the prison through different eyes to our eyes ... I was already out – you know I filed complaints with the Press Council, line by line challenging the reports of the Press, because of their inaccuracies and distortions.*

Fleur de Villiers visits Robben Island

IT IS the view that most disturbs. Spectacular, inescapable – and totally devoid of promise. Table Mountain is an ever-present taunt, the separating strip of sea a metaphor of isolation.

On Robben Island that isolation is complete. And it has little to do with barred windows, locks or the double steel doors that clang behind you as you move into the prison where 370 black men are kept for 'crimes against the state'.

Major-General Jannie Roux, Deputy Commissioner of Prisons, recognises the fact. "Do not expect a five-star hotel," he says at first. "This is a maximum security prison." But a little later: "Even if we were to put a five-star hotel here, it would still be a prison."

For the locks, bars and steel doors, substantial though they are, are in the end only symbols of an isolation so complete that it has put the men behind them out of reach of time and reality. No news is allowed to cross that 9 km stretch of sea.

No change

But for the inmates, their view of the world is as unchanging as the sea and the mountain. For Nelson Mandela, Walter Sisulu, Govan Mbeki, men who once sought to change their world, the world has not changed in 12 years.

The fact of their isolation, its totality, teases the mind. What do they know of the world, of Vietnam, the collapse of the Portuguese empire, of Mozambique, Angola, or Soweto?

The old men of Rivonia are separated from the young boys of Soweto, they can know little of the events which brought their successors to the island.

Mandela, Sisulu, Mbeki, aging and grey, tend the prison garden or wash the windows of their cells and regard the Press with annoyance, contempt or a sneaking amusement. They are here until they die.

But they do not attempt to escape. Perhaps, says General Roux, they believe they can better achieve their goal by staying here. Staying, they study – for what? To kill time, to keep alert and retain some contact, however academic, with the world. Or in the hope of a future beyond the bald statement on their cell doors: Sentence: Life.

At what point does hope die? The answer is pasted to a wall in one of the single cells – a carefully hand-drawn 1977 calendar.

From *The Sunday Times*, 1 May 1977.

Thami Mkhwanazi spent seven years on Robben Island in the 1980s. Three of these years he spent in the same section of the prison as Nelson Mandela. This article tells us about a prisoner's life on Robben Island in the 1980s.

The prisoner who changed the rules

Thami Mkhwanazi

WHEN I met him on the island he had not completely escaped the demands of old age. But he followed a tight schedule. He got up three hours before the warder opened his cell at 7 a.m. He meditated deeply before doing his press-ups ...

Once the door of his 2.5 m square cell was opened he took his toilet bucket and walked down the passage, greeting individual fellow-inmates as he passed their cells towards the section's bathroom.

Revolutionary politics was the order of the day on the island. It was during the cleaning of the buckets that Mandela, his Rivonia Trial colleagues and other prisoners began to engage in political discussion.

Together with the others, Madhiba would take his bucket outside and leave it there for airing. He would immediately run fast around the cement courtyard. Clad in shorts, T-shirt and running shoes, Mandela jogged until he was wet. He then darted into the passage and into his cell, where he grabbed a skipping rope and dashed into a hall used for exercising. A boxer in his youth, he skipped, shadow-boxed, and did a variety of exercises.

Back in the bathroom, he discussed politics while taking a shower of brackish water with other inmates. At breakfast, Madhiba sat on a long communal bench in a row with fellow-inmates ... In the dining hall politics mixed well with soft porridge, bread and coffee.

Notwithstanding the leadership role played by the Rivonia comrades and their being regarded with awe by the authorities and everyone, they were treated no differently from the rest of the prisoners.They too participated in the cleaning of the section.

Mandela engaged in the normal work of scrubbing and polishing floors. When it was his 'span's' turn to scrub the floors, he donned his rubber boots and pushed pools of water with a squeegee.

Mandela's real love was his garden. With the assistance of men like Elias Motsoaledi, Mac Maharaj, Laloo Chiba and Theo Cholo, over the years he cultivated the area around the courtyard, producing tomatoes, cucumbers, melons and chillis.

Cell number 7 in Section B was a hive of activity during the day. His cell was an office, conference room and sleeping quarters. He spent a lot of time talking to fellow-inmates across the ideologies. He was a unifier. As a former lawyer, he was consulted by prisoners.

Madhiba read extensively from a variety of newspapers, including the Afrikaans publications.

Then an LLB degree student, he used to sit quietly in his cell and study. He would rest his mind by sleeping for an hour after a demanding activity. I occupied the back-bench with him and others during the screening of films in the section. He attended virtually all the movie shows, but never lasted through the entire movie.

Like the rest of the prisoners, Mandela came in for his share of punishment for beating the regulations. He was often thrown into the prison within a prison. Along with Walter Sisulu and Govan Mbeki, he was often denied the 'privilege' of study. He was accused of abusing the privilege by using his study pads to write politics.

From *The Weekly Mail*, 16–22 February 1990.

The atmosphere of a university

On one occasion in 1965 when the Commissioner of Prisons came around on an inspection, Nelson Mandela had been asked by those of us who were kept in the isolation section to speak on our behalf about our problems and complaints. The Commissioner of Prisons made one of the most stunning mistakes by asking Nelson in our presence: "Now what is it you want about things like studies, what is it you want?" I'll never forget Nelson's reply: "You should let the atmosphere of a university prevail here on the island." Neville Alexander

Prisoners awarded certificates to one another.

Wiping out illiteracy

With the help of the International Committee of the Red Cross, prisoners were granted permission to teach those who were illiterate – to read and write in their own language, and then to read and write in English.

> *We took people from the lowest level, who came to the island illiterate, and they had to be taught. I remember one group I had – I started with them when they were illiterate – started them up. And by the time they left Robben Island they were able to write letters home – they didn't require anybody to write letters for them, and to address their envelopes. And they spoke English.*
> Govan Mbeki (ANC), sentenced to life imprisonment

Formal education

In 1966 the prison authorities began allowing prisoners to study. People could register either with UNISA for a degree or with Rapid Results College for secondary school education. With the help of teachers such as Dr Neville Alexander, some people who arrived on the island without having completed secondary school left with degrees.

> *Our economics class was a very lively class. Even Suitcase's (the warder) 'Come on, come on!' could never curb its animation ... I wrote my Economic Course 1 papers in Pretoria at the time of my second interrogation and I was praised for my B symbol. Actually the people who deserved praise were my classmates. The discussions we held at the quarry were very helpful.*
> Michael Dingake

The prison authorities saw formal study as a privilege and not a right. This meant that it could be taken away, disrupted or suspended, as a form of punishment.

Political education

> *Many prisoners who went into prison without formal education, came out of prison in some cases with university degrees, formal*

*qualifications ... But more important than these were the many
discussions, seminars, tutorials, lectures that we had which
didn't lead to certification.*

*I remember a discussion on the subject of beauty, which arose
from an item of news we received probably about late 1966.
According to the report, Julius Nyerere, the first President of
independent Tanzania, had banned a planned beauty contest.
This was reported in* Die Burger *or* The Cape Times *and we
managed to smuggle in this particular cutting. This little bit of
news led to a major debate in prison: was Nyerere right or was he
wrong? Is it correct to ban beauty contests? and so on ... I was
commissioned by our inmates to do some research and to write a
discussion document on the theory of beauty ...*
*The point I am making is that that discussion didn't lead to
certification, but it was one of the most useful discussions ...*
Neville Alexander

From the start, the political leadership on the island found ways to
share knowledge on a range of topics. Political education classes
taught people's history. For these classes, papers were written and
circulated via an underground network, and they were preserved,
sometimes by burying them in the soil.

At first this political education was informal and not very
organised. But from the late 1970s the leadership of the different
organisations developed detailed syllabi and courses for the
young militants who were arriving on the island with new ideas
and traditions of struggle.

*A new crop of very young comrades started streaming into the
island. Most of them were MK cadres, but also among them were
BCM (Black Consciousness Movement) members, whose
leadership stated that they had no time 'for the dusty
manuscripts of Marx and Engels'.* Govan Mbeki

So the leadership developed a full academic and education
programme, with materials and study groups.

*If we laid our hands on any book, however thick, it was copied out
and distributed to our membership throughout the various
sections.* Govan Mbeki

Books, magazines, stationery

On a very personal level, I read books in prison which I would never have had the time or the opportunity to read when I was outside: classics of European literature, Gibbon, Shakespeare, the authorised version of the Bible a few times, Dickens; also African history, international law, economics, languages, etc, etc. and of course lots and lots of German literature, which is actually my particular intellectual preoccupation ... I had more banned books inside prison than I had ever had outside. Prisoners are ingenious, they have to be, otherwise things would be very, very difficult. Neville Alexander

Calendars

'... in jail it is the minutes and the hours that are the most difficult to get through. The years go by with relative ease.' (Kathrada, quoting from the book *Mistress of Kafka*)

Calendars, available only in later years, marked the slow passing of time. They were used to record special occasions.

"Fury said to a mouse,
That he met in the house,
'Let us both go to the law:
I will prosecute you –
Come, I'll take no denial;
We must have a trial:
For really this morning
I've nothing to do.'
Said the mouse to the cur,
"Such a trial, dear Sir,
With no jury or judge,
would be wasting our breath."
"I'll be judge, I'll be jury,"
Said cunning old Fury:
"I'll try the whole cause,
and condemn you to death."
From : "Alice in Wonderland."
         Lewis Carrol.

"... as enigmatical as the womb which would never betray [illegible] fruit it was bearing."
Alfred Neuman "The New Caesar"

This prison notebook containing passages and sayings of special meaning, shows extensive reading.

Prisoner's scrapbook.

Sport and recreation

Sport and recreation were very important activities which prisoners fought for on Robben Island. They gave prisoners from different sections a chance to come into contact with one another and to enjoy 'normal' activities in an abnormal environment.

From the late 1960s prisoners formed various clubs, led by sportsmen like Mluleki George and Steve Tshwete. There was a soccer club, rugby club, tennis club and clubs for other sports.

Indres Naidoo describes a football match:

At exactly 8 a.m. on a Saturday morning the cream of the ANC football followers ran onto a small field between the Isolation Block and B Section. Wearing blue prison jerseys were the Rangers, captained by comrade Jacob Zuma, who was serving ten years; the Bucks were in khaki prison shirts, under the leadership of comrade Curnick Ndhlovu, who was serving twenty. I was the referee and, after giving the two teams a talk on discipline and fair play, I signalled the game to begin.

... Watching through the bars on the high strip windows in the Isolation Block were the faces of our leaders: Nelson Mandela, Walter Sisulu, Mac Maharaj, Andrew Masondo, and others.

First we had eight teams in the Makana Football Association, so named after an African leader of resistance who had died a century before, trying to swim to freedom from the island. Four of the teams were composed of PAC prisoners and four of ANC and 'other' prisoners. And we had a committee consisting of two PAC prisoners, two ANC, and one 'other'.

Shortly after that a Referees' Association, a Constitution Committee and a First Aid Unit were also formed. Steve Tshwete was the first chairperson of the Sports Committee. In 1994, after the first democratic elections in South Africa, he was appointed Minister of Sport.

Sports trophy: a soccer ball made by prisoners in the prison workshop.

Prisoner's rugby jersey.

In the 1980s conditions improved and prisoners were allowed to watch TV and films, hire videos, listen to records and form music groups. Choirs were formed, and many prisoners learnt to play musical instruments for the first time, receiving tuition from other prisoners.

Two of the records prisoners listened to on Robben Island.

Contact with the outside world

By the late 1970s prisoners were classified into groups A to D in the same way as in other South African prisons. An A group member was allowed two visits by two people for half an hour each month, and could send and receive three letters a month. A group D prisoner was allowed one visit and one letter a month. All visits were non-contact: the prisoner sat on one side of a cubicle and the visitor on the other, separated by a glass partition.

Letters

Letters are a prisoner's lifeline; not only letters – visits and other channels of communication, photos. In 1966 letters were rare in prison. Most of the political prisoners were still classified as D group. D group were entitled to one letter in three to six months. Few people outside knew of this privilege, since the prison authorities did not always inform them as they were supposed to do. This ignorance meant that some prisoners could receive their first letters after a very long term. Towards the end of 1967 or beginning of 1968, D group prisoners were allowed to receive one letter and one visit a month. Three photos were thrown in to improve and complete prisoner-family contact ... Letters coming in were thoroughly censored; lines were blacked out or cut out. At times the whole contents of the letter were cut out and only the salutation – 'Darling husband' – at the beginning, and the signature at the end were left. Michael Dingake

Visits

Letters were rare, but visits were even rarer. Most of the prisoners were not from the Cape. This meant that their families had to travel a very long way to reach Robben Island, and at great personal cost for only a half-hour visit. Even when prisoners did receive visitors, their conversation was strictly monitored. They were not allowed to talk about anyone who was not part of their family, they were not allowed to mention another prisoner's name and they were not allowed to pass messages to one another.

Helao Shityuwete, a Namibian prisoner, describes a visit from his aunt, who had travelled from Windhoek to see him:

Sitting behind the pane, I was only able to see her head and shoulders. I began shouting greetings to her and she shouted back. Such was the noise from adjacent cubicles that we could hardly hear each other, let alone understand what the other was saying ... We were like lunatics trying to outbid each other. It seemed like just one minute when my 30 minutes of visiting were up. They pulled a board across the window pane and the warder and the policeman in my cubicle grabbed me to take me back to prison ...

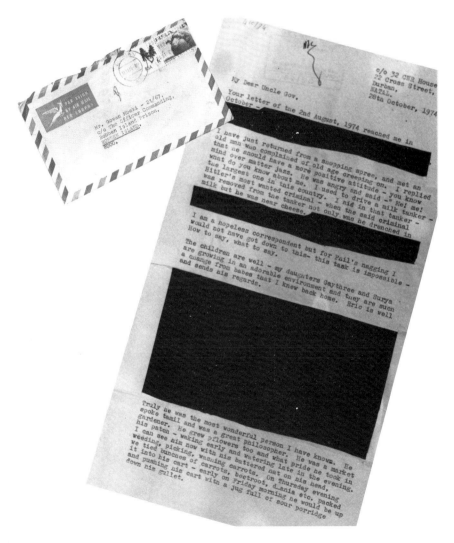

Letters were thoroughly censored.

Children

The thing I missed most was children ... I remember the first time all of us heard children's voices in the quarry. It was as though we had suddenly been struck by lightning. We all of us stood there dead still and everyone was waiting for the moment when we would glimpse the child. Of course it was not allowed. The warders quickly went and made sure we didn't see the kids. But those lone voices, that one occasion in ten years that I heard the voice of a child ... You suddenly realise just how much you are missing ... the emotional deprivation that we were all subjected to. Neville Alexander

One of the things one missed most in prison is children. Complete absence of children. For twenty-three years I had not seen a child ... Ahmed Kathrada

Photos

The presence of pictures of friends and beloved ones in one's cell made a difference, a welcome psychological difference. It helped one survive. Michael Dingake

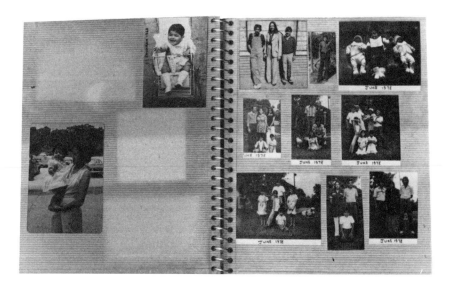

Ahmed Kathrada's photograph album.

News

From 1978 all political prisoners were allowed to listen to censored newscasts which were broadcast over an intercom system. These were not 'live' newscasts, which meant that the authorities could broadcast only those items which they wanted prisoners to hear.

Michael Dingake remembers the first major news item on the intercom system: the report of the death of Sobukwe, the former president of the PAC. Shortly after this, news came through of the massacre of 15 members of the Botswana Defence Force by Ian Smith's troops. To prisoners, it felt as though the news privilege had been granted only to tell prisoners sad news.

Then in 1980, group A prisoners on Robben Island were allowed to buy newspapers for the first time, and these newspapers were to be delivered uncensored. Although this privilege was only extended to group A prisoners, they managed to share their papers and news with the rest of the prisoners.

> *The fear of losing the privilege of buying newspapers did not deter group ones from risking the loss by sharing their papers with groups two and three. It must not be imagined that newspaper subscribers were defiant or careless about preserving their newspapers; no, they tried hard to circulate them by stealth, but the odds were always overwhelmingly against them.* Michael Dingake

Prisoner's radio.

Outside support and solidarity

Solidarity and organisation inside prison helped prisoners survive and fight for better conditions. The resistance of family, friends and organisations outside prison helped prisoners and strengthened their morale. In 1967 prisoners managed to smuggle out reports about their poor conditions and treatment. As a result of these reports, the United Nations, the International Committee of the Red Cross and Helen Suzman managed to get some aspects of prison life improved.

International pressure

As the struggle intensified in South Africa, the ANC in exile called on other countries to impose total sanctions against South Africa. The political struggle in South Africa was placed firmly on the agenda of the international community. Apart from sanctions and disinvestment, grassroots movements in other countries organised protests, rallies and campaigns to highlight the plight of South Africa's political prisoners. In 1988, on Nelson Mandela's 70th birthday, a massive international campaign was launched calling for the release of Mandela and all political prisoners in South Africa.

International opinion and pressure helped prisoners keep up their spirits. Prisoners felt that they were not alone and had not been forgotten. Many individuals and organisations became familiar to prisoners. Among these were: the International Defence and Aid Fund for southern Africa, which publicised the plight of prisoners in apartheid prisons; the United Nations; the anti-apartheid organisations in Britain and elsewhere; the International Red Cross; and Amnesty International.

> *We were particularly encouraged by the news we got of the work being done in the outside world by various anti-apartheid bodies who were keeping the world informed about our conditions on Robben Island. ... Many of us lesser-known prisoners were adopted by groups of Amnesty International.* Indres Naidoo

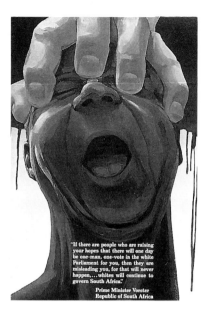

Some of the many posters produced all over the world in protest against apartheid, and in support of the prisoners on Robben Island.

Escape

In 1981 prisoners planned an escape which included air-lifting ANC and SWAPO prisoners off the island on New Year's Day. The plan was not approved by the ANC-in-exile, so it was not carried out.

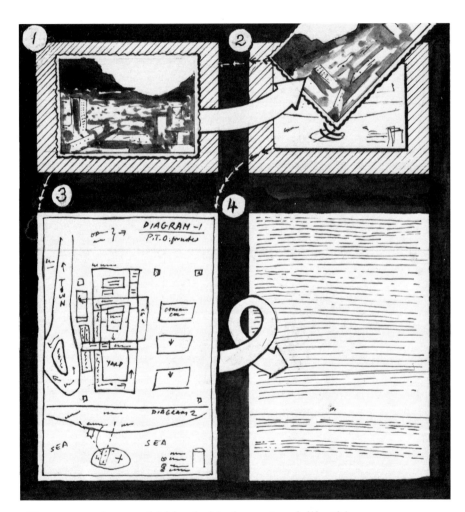

The escape plan was hidden behind a postcard, like this.

In 1982 the Rivonia Trialists were moved from Robben Island to Pollsmoor Prison. Then in 1986 Nelson Mandela wrote to State President Botha and started the negotiations process which led to the unbanning of the liberation movements and eventually to the first democratic national elections in South Africa.

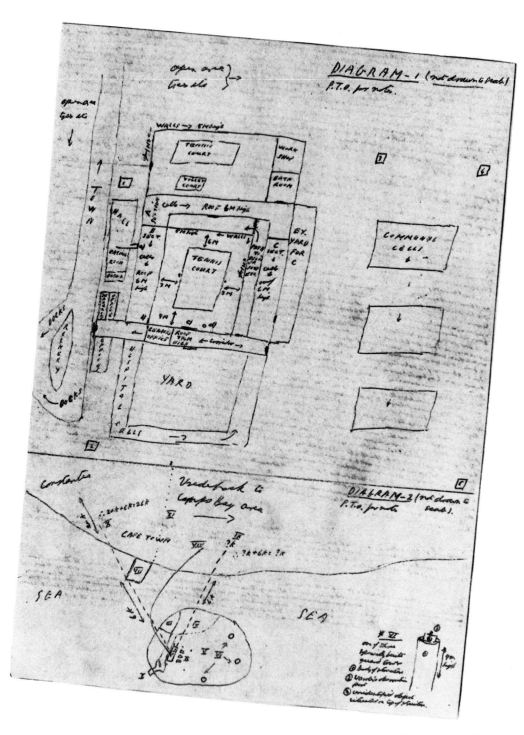

The escape plan.

Leaving Robben Island

The island starts slowly moving back; the reverberations in the boat increase; the engine noise gets louder, and we feel the prison dock being torn from us. We are standing, silent, each at his own porthole, having our last look at what has been our home for ten years ... Goodbye Robben Island ... We turn our attention to Table Mountain, getting bigger and bigger ... The engine noise cuts out, the boat floats along serenely, and we see people moving around on the docks in front of us, some dressed in workers' overalls, others in business suits; the different clothing of a different world in which everything is different, every detail ...
Indres Naidoo

Released prisoners going to the mainland.

People leaving the island with apple boxes containing their possessions.

When people were released from Robben Island, they left carrying
their worldly possessions in cardboard boxes – nearly always
apple boxes. Some of the released prisoners donated their material
to the Mayibuye Centre, and these 'Apple-Box Archives' have
helped to tell the story of Robben Island.

In 1990 Nelson Mandela was released from prison, and in May
1991 the last political prisoners were removed from Robben Island.
When this book was written, in April 1994, the island was still
being used as a prison for common-law prisoners.

Afterword

The future of Robben Island

Robben Island – this small piece of land in Table Bay – has its own tale to tell of the history of South Africa. It is a tale of the lonely exile of the Khoisan, the East Indian prisoners, and the Xhosa leaders of resistance. It is a tale of the isolation of the unwanted – the extremely sick, the poor, the mentally insane and the lepers. It is a tale of the courageous fight for survival by those who opposed apartheid rule. In 1994, the future of this historic island is once again being debated.

- Should the island be developed as a holiday resort?

- Should it become a nature reserve to protect its wildlife?

- Should Robben Island be declared a national monument to preserve its rich history?

- Or should it become a peace institute and a museum?

In May 1994, Nelson Mandela, the new president of South Africa, was sworn into parliament, along with many of his fellow prisoners from Robben Island. Whatever the future holds for this island, it is in the interests of all South Africans to make sure that it never again becomes a place of exile and imprisonment.

Picture credits

We would like to thank all the institutions and individuals that granted us permission to use their photographs. Every effort has been made to trace the copyright holders of photographs and illustrations reproduced in this publication. The publishers will be most grateful for any information regarding the copyright holders of any photographs in this book for which copyright is not credited.

Credits are arranged according to the page on which the picture falls.

10 MC; **11** SAL; **14** SAL; **15** Top and bottom, SAL; **16–17** SAL; **18** Top and bottom, SAL; **19** Top, South African Cultural History Museum; bottom, Horace Coaton; **21** SAL; **22** *The Argus*; **23** Cape Archives; **24** SAL; **25** SAL; **26** Top, Albany Museum, Grahamstown; bottom SAL; **27** Top and bottom, SAL; **28** Top and bottom, SAL; **29** SAL; **30** SAL; **31** SAL; **32** *Cape Times*, SAL; **33** *Cape Times*, SAL; **34** *The Argus*; **36** SAL; **37** MC; **38** MC; **40** MC; **42** MC; **43** MC; **44** MC; **45** *The Argus*; **49** All photographs MC; **50** MC; **51** MC; **53** *The Argus*; **54** Sue Valentine, IDASA; **56** Mike Hutchings; **58** Top and bottom, *The Argus*; **60** Times Media Ltd; **61** *The Argus*; **62** Tracey Derrick, AA, MC; **63** Tracey Derrick, AA, MC; **66** Tracey Derrick, AA, MC; **69** Tracey Derrick, AA, MC; **70** Tracey Derrick, AA, MC; **71** Tracey Derrick, AA, MC; **73** Tracey Derrick, AA, MC; **74** Tracey Derrick, AA, MC; **75** Tracey Derrick, AA, MC; **77** MC; **79** Tracey Derrick, AA, MC; **80** *The Argus*; **81** Mike Hutchings; **83** Newspaper articles, SAL.

Abbreviations
AA Apple-Box Archives
MC Mayibuye Centre, University of the Western Cape
SAL South African Library, Cape Town

The publishers would also like to thank:
Ian Lusted for the illustrations on pages **8–9** and **46–47**, Mara Singer for illustrations on pages **12** and **20**, and Muhdni Grimwood for the illustrations on pages **13** and **78**.

Bibliography

In developing this book we drew on many resources, including the following publications:

Deacon, Harriet; Penn, Nigel; Alexander, Neville *Robben Island: The Politics of Rock and Sand* (Department of Adult Education and Extramural Studies, University of Cape Town, 1993)
Dingake, Michael *My Fight Against Apartheid* (Kliptown, 1987)
International Defence and Aid Fund for Southern Africa and UNESCO *Fighting Apartheid: A Cartoon History* (IDAF and UNESCO, 1987)
International Defence and Aid Fund for Southern Africa *Nelson Mandela: His Life in the Struggle* (IDAF, 1988)
International Defence and Aid Fund for Southern Africa *Nelson Mandela: The struggle is my life* ((IDAF, 1990)
Island in Chains: Ten Years on Robben Island as told by Indres Naidoo to Albie Sachs (Penguin Books, 1982)
Meer, Fatima *Higher than Hope: Rolihlahla We Love You* (Skotaville, 1988)
Reader's Digest Illustrated History of South Africa (Reader's Digest, 1988)
Also the video, *Robben Island Our University*, Lindy Wilson, 1988.

Have you read these books?

From SACHED Books

CHRIS HANI: The Sun That Set Before Dawn
Thami Mali for the SACHED Trust, 1994

Thami Mali, a close friend and comrade of Chris Hani, gives a vivid and moving account of a life devoted to the poor and disenfranchised. Carefully written in accessible English, with photographs.

FREEDOM FROM BELOW
A SACHED/Skotaville book, 1989

Freedom From Below tells of the struggle to organise trade unions in South Africa, from the earliest forms of worker resistance in the 1800s through to the large federations of industrial trade unions today. This book is essential reading for anyone interested in the development of the labour movement in South Africa.

THE NEW AFRICAN HISTORY
A SACHED/Maskew Miller Longman book, 1994

The New African History traces the history of Africa from the stone age through the great states of early Africa, past colonial rule and into Africa's future. In a popular, easy-to-read style this book tackles head-on all the controversial questions. It relates today's hard questions to yesterday's rocky history.

Written by respected academics, *The New African History* is ideal for students, teachers and lecturers, as well as anyone interested in the past, present and future of our continent.

THE STRUGGLE TO TEACH
A SACHED/Maskew Miller Longman book, 1994

This is the story of teachers in South Africa told in their own words. The struggle to teach records tales from around the country – of schools without books or classrooms, of teaching exhausted children who have walked for kilometres to reach school, of battling against a racist education system that is in a state of near-collapse. Teachers speak about their hardships, triumph, anger and dreams.

THE RIGHT TO LEARN
A SACHED/Ravan book, 1992

In this completely revised and updated second edition of her popular and challenging book, Pam Christie examines one of the most crucial issues for South Africa's future – education.

WRITE YOUR OWN HISTORY
A SACHED/Ravan book, 1988

Write Your Own History shows ordinary South Africans how they can write their own history. It helps would-be historians to plan research, use a library, interview people, take notes from books and other written sources, and understand bias in books and newspapers.

Enquiries: SACHED Books, PO Box 11350, Johannesburg 2000
Telephone enquiries: SACHED Books (011) 333-9746

From Mayibuye Books

MZABALAZO: A pictorial history of the ANC
Mayibuye Books in conjunction with the ANC, 1994

Mayibuye History and Literature Series No. 48
Illustrated with more than 80 photographs, many published in this country for the first time, Mzabalazo describes in concise and easy-to-read text the liberation struggle led by the ANC from the year of its foundation in 1912 to the dramatic events leading up to the recent historic elections.

Also available as a portable exhibition consisting of 17 poster-size sheets (594 x 420 mm) suitable for display in schools, libraries, civics and other community centres.

NELSON MANDELA: His life in the struggle
A pictorial history, ex-IDAF London, 1988

Mayibuye History and Literature Series No. 21
This book was prepared as a tribute to President Mandela, then serving his 25th year in prison, on his 70th birthday. Wide international distribution of the book helped inform and intensify the international campaign for his release along with other political prisoners. More than 70 photographs, many not seen in South Africa before, depict Mandela's involvement in the struggle to which he has devoted most of his life.

Also available as a portable exhibition consisting of 14 poster-size sheets (635 x 440 mm) suitable for display in schools, libraries, civics and other community centres.

Enquiries: Mayibuye Centre, UWC, Private Bag X17, Bellville 7535
Telephone: (021) 959 2935 Fax: (021) 959 3411

Book orders: David Philip Publishers, PO Box 23408, Claremont 7735
Telephone: (021) 64 4136 Fax: (021) 64 3358

APARTHEID & THE HISTORY OF THE STRUGGLE FOR FREEDOM IN SOUTH AFRICA
A definitive production on CD-ROM

The Mayibuye Centre is recognised internationally for the importance of its resources and its ongoing work in accessing material and productions relating to the marginalised history and culture of the majority of South Africans.

The latest activity of the Centre is the conversion of complete elements of its collections to CD-ROM format for ease of distribution and access to the disparate elements of its multimedia resources.

The first production in the series is called Mayibuye Books and comprises 50 books, most of which were banned during the apartheid period. Their production, in CD-ROM format provides an excellent tool for all students of contemporary history and politics, as well as social and culture studies.

As with Mayibuye Books, all the future CD-ROM products in the series will cover their specific subject using the full facilities of the medium to search, view and print (where permitted) the text, graphs, photos and other visuals. Using microsoft Multimedia Viewer 2.0, full multimedia facilities are available with a remarkably clear and easy-to-use interface. This provides first-time users of CD-ROM with an easily grasped facility to examine and study the information provided.

Enquiries: Mayibuye Centre, UWC, Private Bag X17, Bellville 7535
Telephone: (021) 959 2935/2954 Fax: (021) 959 3411

Orders: CD-ROM Publications, Suite 9, Ovcon House, Main Road, Constantia, 7800
Telephone: (021) 794 2796 Fax: (021) 794 2797